all about iguanas

mervin f. roberts
and
martha d. roberts

Title Page: A young, healthy specimen of *Iguana iguana*. Note the clear eye, nose not runny, and the absence of sores on the jaws. Photo by G. Marcuse.

Cover photo by John Dommers.

Galapagos Islands iguanas photos on pages 41 and 44 by Lyle Flesher.

9 8 7 6 5 4 3 2 1   **1996 Edition**   9   6 7 8 9

Distributed in the UNITED STATES to the Pet Trade by T.F.H. Publications, Inc., One T.F.H. Plaza, Neptune City, NJ 07753; distributed in the UNITED STATES to the Bookstore and Library Trade by National Book Network, Inc. 4720 Boston Way, Lanham MD 20706; in CANADA to the Pet Trade by H & L Pet Supplies Inc., 27 Kingston Crescent, Kitchener, Ontario N2B 2T6; Rolf C. Hagen Ltd., 3225 Sartelon Street, Montreal 382 Quebec; in CANADA to the Book Trade by Vanwell Publishing Ltd., 1 Northrup Crescent, St. Catharines, Ontario L2M 6P5 ; in ENGLAND by T.F.H. Publications, PO Box 15, Waterlooville PO7 6BQ; in AUSTRALIA AND THE SOUTH PACIFIC by T.F.H. (Australia), Pty. Ltd., Box 149, Brookvale 2100 N.S.W., Australia; in NEW ZEALAND by Brooklands Aquarium Ltd. 5 McGiven Drive, New Plymouth, RD1 New Zealand; in Japan by T.F.H. Publications, Japan—Jiro Tsuda, 10-12-3 Ohjidai, Sakura, Chiba 285, Japan; in SOUTH AFRICA by Lopis (Pty) Ltd., P.O. Box 39127, Booysens, 2016, Johannesburg, South Africa. Published by T.F.H. Publications, Inc.

MANUFACTURED IN THE UNITED STATES OF AMERICA
BY T.F.H. PUBLICATIONS, INC.

CONTENTS

ACKNOWLEDGMENTS

Charles Cole reviewed parts of the manuscript, James Lazell, Jr. suggested some of the diet and taxonomic material, John Meek generously gave his time and thoughts about behavior in captivity, Isabelle Conant provided photographs of several species, Lyle Flesher contributed color photographs he made in the Galapagos Islands, and John Dommers made many of the other color pictures. The authors are grateful to all these people, for without their help there would be no book.

WHY WE WROTE
THIS BOOK

According to the 1974 *International Zoo Yearbook*, published by the Zoological Society of London, the 1971 trade in live reptiles exported from the Republic of Colombia, South America numbered 403,319 specimens. Of this number, 136,993 were common green iguanas. This was the largest number of any single species. There were also 39,892 lizards of other species and 27,727 boa constrictors. Turtles made the bulk of the balance. The biggest buyer was the U.S.A., followed by Germany and Japan.

Now 136,993 iguanas from Colombia alone in one year is a lot of iguanas. Many imported as adults ten years ago with proper care should still be going strong. Although they are good to eat, few if any are eaten. These iguanas are imported solely for the pet trade and the reason is simple. Iguanas are relatively inexpensive, long-lived, hardy, easy to house, easy to feed, colorful, quiet and odorless. They make good pets.

This, then, is a book about all lizards commonly called "iguanas," and the common green one in particular. The chapters do overlap somewhat, and the authors strongly recommend that the readers use the index.

There will be very little about breeding habits because these lizards don't reproduce themselves in captivity, but there will be a rather intensive discussion of diet in both the chapter on food and the chapter on diseases because many of the problems of iguana keeping are really just nutrition problems.

Martha D. Roberts assisted her father (the senior author) in the research leading to this book, and it was she who inter-

Leiocephalus carinatus is a small iguanid lizard sometimes found in petshops which also handle iguanas. Note the twisted tail; this is something an iguana never does. Photo by G. Marcuse.

viewed John Meek in Key West, Florida. Since much of the interview material is being presented intact, and since Mr. Meek's observations cover many aspects of the life of these lizards, the index becomes very important.

Most American readers of this book are accustomed to inches and the Fahrenheit scale of temperature, so all the data, regardless of their source, have been converted to Fahrenheit degrees and inches.

One further note: This book is not written for the scientist but rather for the pet keeper. Not all sources are formally referenced, but some of the texts will be mentioned in passing and the reading list will provide clues for additional study.

Incidentally, a search of the literature unearthed no other single source of detailed information in print for pet keepers about these interesting reptiles. Perhaps this book is the first, and if it is, the authors hope that it will stimulate others more competent to pick up from here and go forward. We discovered that there is a great deal we don't know.

The title of this book creates a slight technical problem which should be cleared up promptly. In the formal classification of living things according to their relationships, we find that among the reptiles there are lizards, and among the lizards there are eighteen families including one called Iguanidae. Now, among these Iguanidae there are more than 50 genera, one of which is called *Iguana*. Within the genus *Iguana* there are only one or perhaps two species. These are the lizards that herpetologists recognize as "true iguanas." Among the other 400 or so Iguanidae we find typical iguanas, chuckwallas, basilisks, fence lizards, anoles (these are the New World "chameleons"), and even the so-called horned toads, more properly identified as horned lizards.

This book is about the true iguanas and the dozen or so species of typical iguanas which resemble them and are also sometimes referred to as iguanas.

The authors assume that most readers just acquired a "true iguana" or are about to, and so the natural history of these attractive animals is presented in terms of helping you make iguana keeping easier and more successful.

The common American green anole, *Anolis carolinensis,* is a member of the family Iguanidae but is not one of the genera of typical iguanas. Photo by Mervin. F. Roberts.

961714

SELECTING A PET IGUANA

A newly hatched iguana is hungry and willing to try eating just about anything it can swallow whole or anything it can tear up and swallow. As they grow older they seem to get set in their ways and more limited in what they are willing to eat. So, if you have a choice, you should choose a small one and assume he still has a tolerant appetite, or be assured before you take him home that in fact he is eating, and precisely what it is that he is eating.

Your choice should be vigorous, active, brightly colored and uninjured. His eyes should be bright and clear and not watery. His tail and nails should be unbroken. The flesh inside his legs and at the base of the tail should be full and firm. Iguanas store a little fat in the base of their tails, and if there is some fat there, it is a good sign. Avoid an iguana which is being force fed or is suffering from a mouth infection. There should be pink healthy flesh in his mouth, with no sores, cottony fungus, or white or yellow spots in his mouth or on his lips. Fluid running from the nose or mouth is a danger sign. Don't take the animal home, especially if you have other reptile pets which might become infected.

Choose a pet which will fit the home you can provide for it. Remember that if you do your job, your iguana will grow. The first few years will be the time of fastest growth and then the rate of growth will decrease, but until the day he dies of old age, a healthy iguana will continue to grow.

NATURAL HISTORY

The authors assume that most of the people who read this will never see a wild iguana in its natural habitat, but we do believe that you will be more successful as a pet keeper if you know what your captive would naturally be accustomed to.

In a book of this size it would be impossible to even refer to all of the published reports about wild and captive iguanas, but a selection from the available literature may provide you with a better insight into your pet, his habits and his needs. You will find a reading list in the back of this book if you wish to delve deeper.

To begin with, most iguanids are hatched from eggs. There is no point in going too far in this line of study here since no pet keeper has yet reported any success in getting his iguanas to reproduce themselves in captivity. Suffice it to say, the eggs of the common green iguana are laid in burrows in the earth. Clutches contain as many as 30 eggs. The soil is generally sandy and near water. One report describes a small island in Gatun Lake, Panama Canal Zone. Very few lizards live on this island, but it seems that 150 or 200 females swim out to the island every year to lay their eggs, mostly in February. The eggs then hatch out, with no help from the adults, at the time the rainy season begins in late April or early May. The young are about eight inches long when they hatch and they soon swim to the mainland.

Females of most lizards store sperm after mating and then remain fertile until they lay their eggs, perhaps several months later. So if your unaccompanied female iguana does lay a clutch of eggs, they might just be fertile. Pack them loosely in damp sphagnum moss or damp clean sand and hold the temperature somewhere between 74° F. and 90° F. Don't turn the eggs as you would birds' eggs but leave them alone. If they are going to hatch, it will happen within perhaps 100 days.

Dr. Richard G. Zweifel at the American Museum of Natural History, New York, developed a technique which is probably even better than that of Mother Nature. He places the eggs on, but not in, the substrate of damp sand or damp moss and the whole within a clear plastic bag. Droplets of water on the inside of the bag assure that the humidity is sufficiently high. The clear plastic permits observation of the development without disturbing the eggs. Dr. Zweifel points out that the bag is kept in normal daylight since darkness only promotes the growth of mold.

It would be neater in a book like this to pin down temperatures and times more precisely, but the best available data just are not that good, and furthermore the incubation period depends only in part upon the temperature.

One account of green iguanas in the arid coastal region of northeastern Colombia states that mating occurs in December with egg laying in March and hatching at the end of May. These iguanas adjusted their activities to keep their body temperature between 96.8° F. and 100.4° F. (Rand, A.S., *Herpet.* 28(3): 252-253; 1972). Another account reports that iguana eggs were found to be incubating naturally between 87.8° F. and 89.6° F. (Mueller, H., *Zool. Beitr.* 18(1): 109-31; 1972). Still another account describes the breeding of an iguana where 70 to 80 days after copulation a female laid 28 eggs which were then incubated at 82.4° F. to 86° F. with 80 to 100% relative humidity. Nine young hatched after 102 to 113 days of incubation (Hun, E., *Salamandra* 8(2): 100-101; 1972). Nine young from 28 eggs is not a particularly good score. Perhaps the temperature was lower than the ideal, or perhaps the male didn't fully accomplish his mission.

The young common green iguanas eat mostly insects, and as they grow their diet shifts to vegetable matter so that a two-pound specimen might be expected to eat perhaps 95% vegetable matter such as leaves, blossoms, buds and fruit. Large common iguanas seem perfectly capable of eating, digesting and thriving on a diet which includes animal protein, but they do not seem to need it the way a juvenile does. Other species from closely related genera, like the rhinoceros iguana, are omnivorous throughout their adult lives.

In the tropics, iguanas are a popular food and are frequently seen in the market places, trussed up and protected against over-heating. They will remain alive without food or water for a long time and thereby provide fresh meat without refrigeration. In northern Latin America the common iguana is called *gallina de palo*—chicken of the tree. The eggs are considered a delicacy, and in iguana stew the eggs from a gravid female are added to the meat.

Archie Carr, one of the world's most prominent herpetologists, describes a recipe for iguana stew, beginning at the beginning with "Catch a fat female iguana, preferably in March or April, kill it and skin it and remove the insides. . ." He goes on to remind the cook to save all the eggs, the liver and the heart. After cutting up the carcass it should be browned lightly in coconut oil, covered with water and flavored with garlic and a chili piquante. The mature eggs should be boiled in salty water flavored with a chili pepper for one half hour, then drained and added to the stewed meat. The diced liver, yellow eggs and heart should also be added at this time and cooking should continue until most of the liquid is gone. The remaining liquid should be poured over red beans and rice and the stewed meat heaped on top.

Coming back to the habits of the iguana, it might be mentioned here that still another name—the tree iguana—is sometimes applied to *Iguana iguana*, and for good reason. These animals seem to be more arboreal than terrestrial. The fruits, flowers, buds and leaves they eat are all available from the "safe" elevation of a tree limb. Other smaller lizards they might eat are also arboreal. The iguana seems to think—if he is capable of that much thinking—that he is safer in a tree than on land, so he is much easier to capture from a tree than if he is on the ground.

Under perfect conditions from the point of view of an iguana or to a greater degree a basilisk, his tree might well overhang water. Then if threatened in the tree, he will drop directly into the water and swim on the surface or under water

11

Iguana iguana iguana — the primary subject of this book. Notice the large scale on the lower jaw under the ear and the rings' of scales around the body and tail. This is a juvenile certainly less than three years old. Photo by Isabelle Hunt Conant.

to safety. A green iguana has no trouble remaining hidden under water for a half hour to evade an enemy.

Ideally your pet might grow to six and one-half feet (mostly tail) and a weight of perhaps twenty or thirty pounds. A male tends to be larger, more brightly colored and longer spined than a female. Most pet keepers don't know the sex of their specimens and it really doesn't matter.

Records of ten or twelve years in captivity are not very unusual, and with intelligent care on your part your pet may do at least this well.

A PLACE IN THE SUN

The common green iguana is one species within one genus of a family of lizards found mostly in the New World. This green iguana and the other typical iguanas are tropical and semi-tropical and active during daylight hours (diurnal). Their eyes have round pupils and well developed lids. Their tongues are short, thick and only slightly notched, as contrasted to the long forked tongue of, for instance, the monitor lizards. It lays eggs in common with most other iguanids (oviparous). Only a few give birth to living young (viviparous). They are frequently but not always brightly colored; they often have spines, frills or crests, and many can distend their throats. They can alter their color somewhat, some species more than others. Some may favor trees (arboreal) and others favor the land (terrestrial). Two are from the Galapagos Islands, and one of these is semi-marine, eats seaweed and would probably rather die than climb a tree.

For a beginning herpetologist or hobbyist pet keeper, the best iguana is the common green iguana—scientifically: *Iguana iguana iguana*. If you don't go out of your way when you choose a pet in a pet shop, this is what you probably will get. Good. The only other iguanas that resemble it are *Iguana iguana delicatissima* which lacks the circular shields found below the eardrums of *Iguana iguana iguana*, and *Iguana iguana rhinolopha* which has a slight protuberance at the snout. So there you have it—genus *Iguana*, species *iguana*, and subspecies perhaps *iguana* or *delicatissima* or *rhinolopha*.

For a better understanding and another opinion of the relationship between what laymen call "*Iguana delicatissima*" and "*rhinolopha*," read James D. Lazell, Jr., 1973, "The

Lizard Genus *Iguana* in the Lesser Antilles," *Bulletin of the Museum of Comparative Zoology*, Harvard University, Cambridge, Massachusetts, Volume 145, Number 1. Lazell is satisfied that there are two species, *I. iguana* and *I. delicatissima*, and further that "*rhinolopha*" is not a valid species but rather that some iguanas just happen to have horn-like scales on their snouts. Dr. Lazell goes on in this 28-page illustrated dissertation to describe not only the structural features of these animals but also their natural history, and he makes an important point for pet keepers by remarking that he has seen wild iguanas eating birds' eggs and carrion, but never papaya or citrus fruits.

Iguana iguana "rhinolopha". This may not be a valid subspecies. The long spines are found only on mature specimens. Photo by G.E. Burghardt.

The name iguana according to the eleventh edition of the *Encyclopedia Britannica* is derived from the Spanish equivalent of the Carib Indian name for these lizards, *iwana*. This name—iguana—was applied in 1825 to a fossil of a giant extinct herbivorous reptile, the *Iguanodon*. The *Iguanodon*, an extinct contemporary of the dinosaurs, and its modern namesake have in common a peculiar form of tooth, being round at the root and blade-like with serrated edges towards the tip. The teeth are described as pleurodont—that is, they are fastened to the inner surface rather than the top edge of the lower jaw.

This business of systematically classifying iguanas gets sticky, and with the aim of clarifying the issue you might want to refer to the informal arrangement in the next chapter. Bear in mind that this book is primarily about the true iguana, *Iguana iguana*, and in passing we will make reference to the dozen or so typical iguanas.

TRUE IGUANAS AND A SELECTED LIST OF TYPICAL IGUANAS

Starting at the top we have: —

Kingdom—Animalia—Animals. This eliminates plants and lower forms of life.

Phylum—Chordata—With a backbone or at least a dorsally located central nervous system. This eliminates worms, molluscs, insects, etc.

Class—Reptilia—Cold-blooded, with lungs, hatched on land. This eliminates fish, amphibians, birds and mammals.

Order—Squamata—The scaly ones, but eliminating crocodilians, turtles and beak-heads (Rhynchocephalia).

Suborder—Sauria—Just lizards. This eliminates snakes.

Family—Iguanidae—One of 18 families of lizards. These have pleurodont teeth.

Genus—Those listed below are frequently judged to *look like* iguanas.

GENUS	NUMBER OF SPECIES
Amblyrhynchus	1
Conolophus	1
Iguana	1 separated into 3 subspecies
Brachylophus	1
Cyclura	5, more or less
Ctenosaura	5

Enyaliosaurus	2
Hoplocercus	1
Dipsosaurus	4, more or less
Sauromalus	6
Basiliscus	4

Now let's review the species which you might encounter or hear about.

AMBLYRHYNCHUS — One species, the Galapagos Islands marine iguana, *Amblyrhynchus cristatus.* Impossible to keep captive since it lives near seawater and eats only certain seaweeds. Darwin wrote about them in some detail and nowadays zoologists round out their careers with books describing their pilgrimage to this fountainhead of zoological knowledge. But for the pet keeper, NO. Length, four and a half feet. Weight,

Amblyrhynchus cristatus, the marine iguana of the Galapagos. This is the creature that captivated the imagination of the great Charles Darwin. Photo by G. Marcuse.

The Galapagos land iguana, *Conolophus subcristatus,* is frequently seen in zoos but rarely in private collections. It is protected by law. Photo by G. Marcuse.

twenty-two pounds. There is a subspecies, *A.c. venustissimus,* found only on Hood Island. It is only 30 inches maximum length and brightly colored, but nevertheless is valueless as a captive pet.

CONOLOPHUS — One species, the Galapagos land iguana, *Conolophus subcristatus.* It is a vegetarian, eating shoots, bark, flowers, fruits, cactus pads and grasshoppers. With a row of spines down the back, this is a powerful looking lizard; however, it is easy to tame. It needs warmth—say 80° to 90° F. It is surely used to salty food and may actually relish it. Four feet long.

17

Close-up of a mature Galapagos land iguana. Notice especially the bumpy scales on the head and the spines at the back of the neck. Photo by G. Marcuse.

IGUANA — The primary subject of this book. Depending on whose classification—and when it was written—there is one species or two and perhaps even three subspecies. For purposes of this book there is one species with three subspecies all having identical natural history and only slight differences in appearance.

IGUANA IGUANA IGUANA — Common green iguana, tuberculated iguana, common iguana, chinese dragon and, in Central America, *gallina de palo*—chicken of the

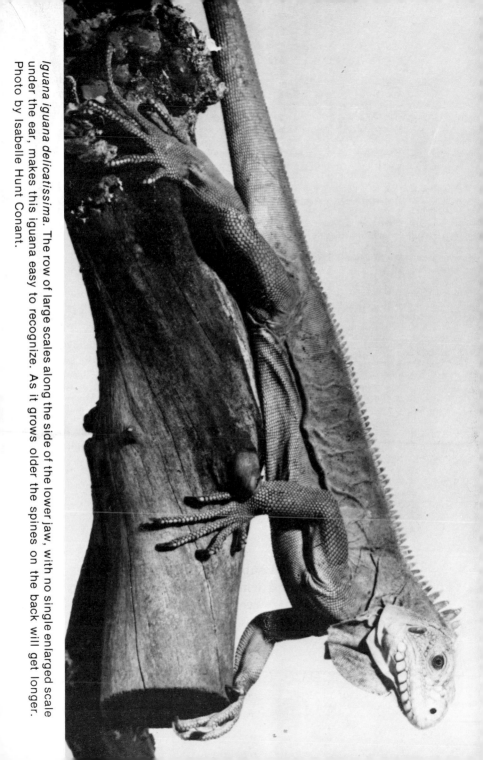

Iguana iguana delicatissima. The row of large scales along the side of the lower jaw, with no single enlarged scale under the ear, makes this iguana easy to recognize. As it grows older the spines on the back will get longer. Photo by Isabelle Hunt Conant.

tree. Maximum recorded length, six feet seven inches and a weight of thirty pounds. Distributed today over Mexico, Central America, tropical South American and several islands of the West Indies. They seem to survive but not necessarily reproduce themselves on several Florida Keys.

IGUANA IGUANA DELICATISSIMA — A subspecies, variety, or race, this lizard differs from *Iguana iguana iguana* in that *delicatissima* lacks the large circular shield beneath each ear drum.

IGUANA IGUANA RHINOLOPHA — The third "variety" is found in Mexico. It differs from the others in that it has several erect spines on its snout. It also has, unders its ears, the circular shields of *Iguana iguana iguana*. The size, habits and general appearance of all three are otherwise the same.

Cyclura macleayi caymanensis is an unusual iguana which may never appear in petshops but is perhaps available from herpetologists. Photo by Muller-Schmida.

Cyclura cornuta.
Photo by Muller-
Schmida.

CYCLURA CORNUTA — Rhinoceros iguana, also formerly called *Metopocerus cornutus.* Santo Domingo (Haiti and the Dominican Republic).Three blunt horns on the snout, a stout body and a row of spines down its back. Dark brown to dull grey. Dangerous when wild but readily tamed, it will eat from its owner's fingers. Requires some animal food—a small chicken or pigeon or a road killed rabbit or squirrel now and then should round out its mostly fruit and vegetable diet nicely. Unfortunately the species is endangered.

CYCLURA CARINATA — Turks Island iguana. Turks and Caicos Islands. Three feet. Smaller but similar to rhinoceros iguana.

CYCLURA BAEOLOPHA — Bahama iguana. Bahamas, Jamaica, and perhaps Cuba. Four feet. Another smaller version of the rhinoceros iguana but lacking horns on the snout. It does not climb trees. Dangerous when wild. Endangered.

This juvenile *Ctenosaura* is perhaps the species *C. acanthura*. *Ctenosaura* species are often common but are difficult to identify. Notice how small the scales along the lower jaw are compared to *Iguana*. Photo by G. Marcuse.

An adult specimen of the Mexican black iguana, *Ctenosaura acanthura*. Photo by Isabelle Hunt Conant.

Ctenosaura pectinata, one of the several spiny-tailed iguanas. This may possibly also be known under one or more alternate scientific names — *Ctenosaura* is a very confused genus. Photo by Isabelle Hunt Conant.

BRACHYLOPHUS FASCIATUS — A "typical" but not "true" iguana. The Fiji Island iguana, handsome, rare, three feet, vegetarian.

CTENOSAURA HEMILOPHA — Common spiny-tail iguana. Central Mexico to U.S. border. Three feet. Grey black with a short spiny tail. Spends more time on the ground than the common green iguana and requires more animal food. Robust and dangerous. This species was formerly called *Ctenosaura conspicuosa*, the banded spiny-tail iguana.

Ctenosaura hemilopha. Don't argue about the proper name of this iguana with an expert! Photo by G.E. Burghardt.

CTENOSAURA ACANTHURA — Black iguana. Mexico and Central America. Can run on two feet. More terrestrial than arboreal. Young specimens are uniformly bright emerald green. This is a spiny-tailed iguana and may in fact by the very same species as *Ctenosaura hemilopha.*

CTENOSAURA MULTISPINIS — Black spiny-tail iguana. Mexico. Probably the very same as *C. acanthura* but described by another scholar.

ENYALIOSAURUS — Two species from Mexico. Uncommon in the pet trade.

This Mexican spiny-tailed iguana, *Enyaliosaurus clarki*, is more of a desert animal than the typical rainforest iguana. Note the flattened tail. Photo by Isabelle Hunt Conant.

The uncommon Brazilian club-tailed iguana, *Hoplocercus spinosus,* somewhat resembles *Enyaliosaurus* but has a shorter tail. Photo by G.E. Burghardt.

HOPLOCERCUS SPINOSUS — Club-tailed iguana. A Brazilian species, terrestrial, and an eater of grubs, termites and mealworms. Difficult to maintain in captivity.

DIPSOSAURUS DORSALIS — Desert iguana, crested lizard, northern crested lizard. Southwestern U.S. and northern Mexico. Eighteen inches. Eats flowers of cactus and other desert plants. Base color is light cream with dark maroon markings. Gentle. Reported to eat dandelions, geranium flowers and lettuce. Needs desert heat and light.

DIPSOSAURUS CARMENENSIS — Carmen Island crested lizard, Carmen Island, Gulf of California. Mentioned for the record only.

DIPSOSAURUS CATALINENSIS — Santa Catalina Island crested lizard, Santa Catalina Island, Gulf of California. Mentioned for the record only.

Sauromalus obesus, the chuckwalla, makes an interesting pet in the desert terrarium. It is protected by law in many areas. Photo by L. van der Meid.

The desert or "crested" iguana, *Dipsosaurus dorsalis*, has an inconspicuous crest of spines on the back. The very short snout, rounded head, longer toes, and color pattern with long black lines and white spots distinguish it from the chuckwalla. Photo by L. van der Meid.

Basiliscus basiliscus, the agile iguana that "walks on water". Photo by G. Marcuse.

Close-up of the head of *Basiliscus basiliscus*. The crest is especially conspicuous. Photo by G. Marcuse.

SAUROMALUS — Chuckwallas. There are six species in the genus which *might* be called iguanas. The six species are found in deserts of the southwestern United States and Mexico and are not discussed elsewhere in this book since they are not very typical.

BASILISCUS — A genus of northern South America, Central America and tropical Mexico. There are four species all commonly called basilisks. They grow up to three feet long, mostly tail, and the males are especially attractive with a high crest on the back and tail or a rooster-like comb on the back of the head. The basilisks are arboreal and extremely agile. All four species are primarily insectivorous and favor mealworms, caterpillars, grubs, mice and small birds. The point to remember here is *extreme agility*. They are not especially typical iguanas in view of their extreme agility and diet, but any pet keeper who frequents shops dealing with iguanas will eventually see one. The basilisk is so fast that he is sometimes able to run across the surface of water. A small specimen can travel some distance on water before breaking the surface tension and falling through, only to continue its travel by swimming. The basilisk can run on its hind legs, and this trait, coupled with its ability to travel short distances *on* water, have given it the colloquial name in Panama of Jesus lizard. Close examination of the basilisk's feet will disclose specialized scales which help it keep from breaking through the surface.

Also to be noted for the record only are two genera from Madagascar, *Hopluras* with five species and *Chalarodon* represented by one species.

The spread dewlap or throat pouch is a sign that the iguana is irritated or upset by something. Since iguanas are seldom belligerent to people under normal circumstances, the dewlap of a pet is seldom spread. Photos by John Dommers.

ENDANGERED SPECIES

A recent edition of the *Red Data Book* by H.E. Honegger for the International Union for Conservation of Nature and Natural Resources, Survival Service Commission, Zurich, Switzerland (1968) lists the following typical iguanas as endangered species:

Andros Island ground iguana or Bahama iguana, *Cyclura baeolopha* (Bahamas)
Rhinoceros iguana, *Cyclura cyclura cornuta* (Santo Domingo)
Grand Cayman iguana, *Cyclura macleayi lewisi* (Jamaica)
Ricord's ground iguana, *Cyclura ricordi* (Santo Domingo)
Watling's Island ground iguana, *Cyclura rileyi* (Bahamas)

As you can see, some are so rare they are not mentioned in the *Selected List of Typical Iguanas* in this book. Since no one breeds these animals, capture and ownership of these endangered species will guarantee their ultimate destruction.

Opposite:
The horns on the snout are the obvious origin of the common name rhinoceros iguana for *Cyclura cornuta*. Most species of this genus are endangered, so they are seldom available as pets. There is also much controversy as to the proper names for the species; many are found only on small, isolated Caribbean islands. Photo by Isabelle Hunt Conant.

The head scalation of *Iguana iguana* is a marvel in intricate detailing. Every scale is very constant in position and size. Lizard species are often based on small but constant differences in number of scales below the eye, size of the scales between the eyes, and other seemingly minute but very useful characters. Photo by John Dommers.

The spines of the dorsal crest of *Iguana iguana* seem to grow from enlarged scales along the midline of the body. Generally spines are larger in adults than in juveniles, but their tips are often broken and partially regenerated. Photo by John Dommers.

YOU AND YOUR IGUANA

This chapter should give you some understanding of your iguana's thinking processes, responses, intelligence and how he demonstrates these traits as your captive. Iguanas are tropical, herbivorous, solitary, stupid, arboreal, long-lived, quiet, diurnal, sexually dimorphic (but unresponsive in captivity) and able to let go of part of their tail to escape enemies when all else fails.

Let's consider iguana habits in terms of successful petkeeping. To begin with, they are tropical and cold blooded. This means that to thrive they must be warm most of the time. If not, they cannot properly digest their food. Evenings and nights at 75° F. are okay so long as there are at least several hours every day of at least 85° F. Shade and/or a cool bath should be available to permit the animal to make his own choices. Your pet needs moisture to help shed and, since this is a continuous process, moisture—a bath or a spray—should be available frequently, but your pet should not be kept wet.

Herbivorous as mature adults, they start out eating animal matter. Most authorities agree they *need* very little *animal* protein after they mature. They are known to enjoy cooked eggs, cooked anchovies and canned dog food, and it is surely good for them, but they will also do very nicely on a 100% fruit and vegetable diet. In that case the vegetables should include high protein beans and peas and fatty avocados as well as the staple bananas and vegetables.

Iguanas don't rely on each other for defense or companionship, having no "pack of wolves" or "flock of birds" behavior. They get along with each other, frequently crowding onto a perch but seemingly ignoring each other totally. When the

38

females dig their burrows to lay eggs, each female common green iguana digs her own burrow. When an iguana catches an insect or finds a piece of fruit, he doesn't share; he eats it alone. So, for the pet keeper or the iguana it doesn't matter whether there is just one or several.

Iguanas learn very little—and slowly at that. They have no oral communication. Birds tweet, frogs croak, bees buzz, lions roar, but iguanas barely hiss, rarely display their dewlaps and hardly do more than quietly munch their food. They do develop travel patterns. As house pets they will follow the sun around a room, go to the bathroom to defecate on paper after taking a bath and climb into a warm dark cage to sleep at night, but that is about the limit of how they demonstrate what they may be thinking. A wild iguana is smart enough to swim underwater to avoid a dog or coatimundi, and he will remain underwater as long as a half hour and perhaps come up in another place to confound a waiting predator. He is dumb enough to be caught in a noose when he is in a tree. An iguana on land seems ill at ease, nervous, alert and ready to run at the slightest provocation, but the same animal in even a low tree will feel so at ease as to be easily captured.

In the wild, our typical iguana was eight inches long when hatched from an egg which had been deposited in a tunnel in a sandy hillside. He grew up with no parental care and little or no association with other iguanas. He inherited or acquired a strong fear or hatred of dogs and dog-like animals. He feels secure in the height of a tree or in water (where he can remain submerged for as long as a half hour). He started life eating plant and animal food, the animal life being predominantly insects. He quickly became a creature of habit. If his food was mostly fruit, he probably will prefer to eat fruit for the rest of his life. If it was mostly flowers, soft leafy vegetables and pea or bean type things, then probably he will prefer to continue to enjoy these things or something which resembles them. If his diet as a juvenile was well mixed, it is possible that this habit will continue. Mr. Meek in Florida has iguanas which thrive on a diet of bananas and hibiscus flowers. In Washington, D.C. the senior author saw a 13-year-old iguana which lived most of its life in an apartment warmed by a radiator and irradiated by

In *Iguana iguana* and some of the other iguanas the neck is protected by enlarged scales developed as pointed heavy thorns or tubercles. Photo above by H. Hansen, Aquarium, Berlin; that below by John Dommers.

The relatively colorful marine iguana of Hood Island, *Amblyrhynchus cristatus venustissimus*.

Galapagos marine iguanas form gigantic basking colonies on the rocky shores of the islands.

an ultraviolet lamp one half hour or so daily. This apartment dweller is four feet long and certainly weighs more than ten pounds. It is thriving, but it probably never tasted a hibiscus flower. It does, however, enjoy spinach souffle — served hot. Don't laugh — one fine large specimen was donated to a zoo when it outgrew its home. The donor told the zoo curator that it had been eating — get this — mozzarella cheese and ice cream! Still another specimen was reported to eat anchovy pizza. This is not a chapter on diet, but the digression is intended to suggest that habits dictate iguana eating behavior, but the final results are liable to surprise you.

What goes in must come out, and here the iguana has habits which you can apply to train your pet to drop his leavings in the same place every time. First, your pet will probably want to defecate at about the same time every day once his eating pattern and temperature are established. Second, if he is in water (or remembers that he had been in water in a certain place) this may trigger activity. Eventually, with some intelligent patience on your part, you should be able to train him to relieve himself once every day or two on a piece of dampened newspaper in the bottom of a dry bathtub. If your pet is always caged, you can concentrate on other problems, but lifetime caging presents another thing for you to think about—that is, exercise. Your pet should be able to walk, climb and flex his muscles.

Once you establish the territorial limits within which your pet is free to move, patterns will be established. If you give your pet the freedom of a room or several rooms, he will soon be at one place to sleep at night—dark and confining perhaps. He will defecate when he awakes, perhaps not every day, but in the same place however often. Perhaps he will choose a pad of newspaper which has been dampened on top. "Perhaps" is not the key word, but it is not to be forgotten. What means a lot to one iguana might no mean as much to another individual—but let's get on. He may expect to be fed at the same place; soon you will recognize his hunger signals. He may snort and create a small sound from his nose as he discharges a small quantity of fluid from his nostrils. This fluid evaporates to leave salt-like crystals, but it is the act of snorting, in one example known to the senior author, which perhaps suggests that your pet is ready to be fed. Maybe yours will perform this little act near the refrigerator, if it is your habit to feed him from there.

Your voiceless pet may also display annoyance with a stranger by opening his mouth. Not attacking or biting or hissing, but simply opening his mouth. An iguana is not much for emotional outbursts, and in fact you will be challenged to notice the messages from your pet. If there are any at all, they will be subtle and quiet, certainly not the chatter of a parakeet, the bark of a dog or even the hiss of a snake. The only really violent emotional display you might witness would come if your pet were on the floor in the middle of the room (with no place to hide) and he suddenly spied a dog. He probably would turn his body to present his tail as a whip, and a dangerous weapon it is. In a real emergency he might even let go of his tail in order to escape if all else failed.

Later in the day your pet might choose a warm sunny window sill, a radiator or radiator cover to soak up a little heat. If he is well fed, warm and feels safe from enemies, he won't be much of a wanderer or acrobat. Remember, this animal is a vegetarian, not a hunter of anything more mobile than perhaps a snail or a mealworm.

How about his relationship with you? Well, he will enjoy you most when the room is cold and your body temperature is more to his liking than the floor behind the sofa or the shelf of the bookcase. He will enjoy you when you rub his head, mostly when he is shedding his skin and a patch over one eye is itching him. Affection? No. Live with humans? Yes.

Your dog might live *for* you, but your iguana will at most live *with* you. He will eat from your fingers if he is hungry and sit in your lap or on your shoulder if he is cold, certainly spectacular actions but not necessarily affectionate.

William Beebe, who was director of tropical research for the New York Zoological Society for many years, reported on what he believed was an intelligent act by a Galapagos land iguana. He saw one walk up to a cactus and strike the base of the plant several times. Soon two pieces of fruit fell, but before the cactus knocker could collect his prizes, another of the same species rushed up and swallowed both. Whole. The knocker

Although similar to the marine iguana, the Galapagos land iguana, *Conolophus subcristatus,* has a somewhat more pointed and smoother head.

Although once common, rhinoceros iguanas, *Cyclura cornuta,* have been reduced in numbers by destruction of their habitat and over-collecting. Photo by Sherman A. Minton.

The only species of the large *Cyclura* iguanas likely to be seen today even in most zoos is *Cyclura cornuta*. Easily recognized by the large size and the usually prominent snout horns, the skin at the back of the skull between the ears is also greatly thickened in this species. If cornered it can put up a good and dangerous fight. Photo by H. Hansen, Aquarium Berlin.

then bit the thief's foot and the thief ran off. Now Beebe was actively observing tropical animal life for forty years and this was the most intelligent iguana activity he was able to report. Draw your own conclusions.

Your pet can be expected to respond in ways you can measure to warmth, light, food, dogs, and water, but you will need a lot of patience and a sharp eye to spot many of these responses.

When in trouble, an iguana heads for a tree or for water. The ideal escape would be up a tree overhanging water, then to drop into the water, swim underwater and quietly come to the surface sometime later. If things get worse, and only as a last resort, the iguana can drop most of his tail. The discarded appendage will swish about for a while and perhaps distract the enemy while the reptile makes his escape. The tail stump will bleed a little then heal and slowly regenerate, but it will never be as nice as the original. There will be a scar line and the new tail will probably be solid black rather than black-banded green, and possibly it will not be as long as the original. *C'est la vie!*

Common iguanas are arboreal. They like to live in trees. They *could* spend their entire adult lives in trees, the females coming down once a year to dig burrows in a sandy hillside to lay eggs and the young remaining on land until they get too large or slow or hungry to subsist on just crickets and smaller reptiles. Your pet should be permitted to climb and perch and feel secure on a high window sill, valance or mantle piece. He can manage without the water under the perch if you provide a place to bathe or soak once in a while.

Longevity records for iguanas suggest that ten years for a common green iguana is not at all unusual. One pet kept in an apartment is known by the author to be over twelve years old. W. Michael Carey of the University of South Florida, Tampa, reported on two caged pets, one of which lived twelve years and five months; when it died it measured about 13½ inches from snout to vent. Since the tail might be more than three-fifths the total length, we could estimate a total length of perhaps four feet. Another captive lived ten years and five months; its snout-vent length (SVL) was about twelve inches, thus making a nearly four-foot reptile. One reason for the SVL standard measurement is that all lizards have snouts and vents but many don't have intact original tails.

These iguanas were housed in a cage with tree limbs. The cage was nearly seven feet long and over four-and-a-half feet high. They were fed mixed fruits and vegetables three times a week, and bonemeal with multiple vitamins (ABDEC) was offered once weekly. Carey also reported on a pair of desert iguanas, *Dipsosaurus dorsalis*, which died accidently after fourteen years and seven months of captivity. Their size suggested that they may have been more like twenty years old at the time of their death.

Although the scarred scales of the lower jaw indicate that this specimen of *Iguana iguana* was at one time poorly treated, it is now healed and in excellent health. Photo by Van Raam.

Cyclura baeolopha has one of the largest natural distributions of the Caribbean island iguanas, being known from at least the Bahamas and Jamaica and perhaps also being found in Cuba. As usual with this genus, it is seldom seen as a pet and is too large for the average household anyway. Photo by H. Hansen, Aquarium Berlin.

The relatively small *Cyclura carinata* is restricted to the Turks and Caicos Islands between the Bahamas and Hispaniola. Photo by Sherman A. Minton.

Cyclura macleayi caymanensis. Photo by Sherman A. Minton.

Iguanas hiss at dogs if they can't escape. Otherwise they are quiet—pet keepers hear the curtains and drapes tearing as their pet tries to climb, but that is about the limit of their noise making.

One activity of common iguanas which might be classed as a noise is the snort which accompanies the clearing of salty fluid from the nostrils. Apparently this is how iguanas regulate the salt content in their bodies. It is through an organ in their snouts that they accumulate a briny fluid which they snort out from time to time.

Common green iguanas are more awake than asleep during the day and they do sleep at night. They like to sleep in a "safe" place—possibly enclosed and surely elevated. Many house pet iguanas get their owners to furnish them with an upper bookshelf or a board mounted over a window. For a lizard this is quite an accomplishment, but to get a shelf built proves how easily people can be trained by iguanas.

Mature common green iguanas are sexually dimorphic. That is, you may be able to determine their sex by their general appearance. Males are brighter colored, larger and their spines are longer (except in juveniles, where males and females all look alike). Below the earhole, *I.i. iguana* has a large colorful scale—call it a shield; on the adult male this shield is relatively larger than on a same-size female. Also, only females lay eggs. For reasons unknown to pet keepers, iguanas do not reproduce in captivity. In fact, they display hardly any sexual behavior.

Both sexes have long tapering round tails. The tails are at least three-fifths of their total length. Both sexes have the same black ring pattern around the green tail, and both sexes use their tails as weapons. An adult six-foot iguana could probably break a smallish dog's leg by a blow from its tail. Certainly a formidable weapon, even in those species where it is not spiny.

Incidentally, if you wish to capture an iguana with its tail intact, try to capture it with a noose on a pole. A fishing rod might work, with some stiff monofilament leader for the looped noose. Catch the animal about its neck and avoid handling the tail or the back near the tail. Not easy since it will probably thrash about. The iguana trade is a specialty of young Latin American boys; don't deprive them of their fun.

JOHN MEEK INTERVIEW

John Meek has been raising and taming iguanas on the Florida Keys since 1970. He has three as pets now and has probably handled 70 in the course of his hobby. Strangely, he cannot distinguish any individual personality in his three pets. Yet when he was offered $100 for a particular iguana he had owned for some time and for which he had paid $8, he would not sell it.

It usually takes a week for Mr. Meek to tame an iguana. When one no longer whips its tail about or attempts to bite, he considers it tame. After that, it will not bite a human unless squeezed or otherwise abused. He knows of one iguana that was teased and poked by children until it became nasty and had to be released. It is now living on No Name Key and was reported to be frequenting a large ditch there. He has read that they will "revert to nature" if they are returned to their original habitat. Experience has shown, however, that with proper handling they will become more docile, dependent and lazy the longer they are cared for.

The first step in Mr. Meek's taming process is the creation of a custom-made harness. This is made of leather in the shape of an "H". The straps straddle the iguana's forelegs and fasten over each shoulder blade with a buckle. The straps will be connected with an additional band of leather if the iguana becomes squirmy. He attaches the harness to a fishing line on a cut-off deep sea fishing pole. Then he lets the iguana run and swim until it tires, which usually takes about a half hour for each exercise period. Next, he holds it as he would a snake, with its head between his forked fingers, then takes it with the other hand, again with its head between his fingers, but this time

Ctenosaura hemilopha. This close-up clearly shows the spiny scales placed in rings around the tail, making the tail a very effective defensive weapon. Photo by F.J. Dodd, Jr.

An open mouth exposing pink or white gums and mouth cavity is a common threat display in iguanas. Photo of *Ctenosaura pectinata* by Sherman A. Minton.

The "bloody nose" of this basilisk, *Basiliscus basiliscus*, indicates it has not yet adapted to captivity and is still trying to escape. Photo by H. Hansen, Aquarium Berlin.

The desert iguana, *Dipsosaurus dorsalis*, is one of the few true iguanas found in the United States, where it occurs in the deserts of the southwestern states. Photo by F.J. Dodd, Jr.

with its chest on his palm. Then with the free hand he soothes the top of its head gently with one finger. In time its eyes will close and it will become so relaxed that Mr. Meek can move the head or a leg without the slightest response. Some seem to like being fondled under the head, some do not.

Usually he spends an hour with the iguana in the morning, some time at various intervals during the day, and an additional hour in the evenings. It never takes him more than a week to tame even the older ones, and he has tamed one in 3½ days. The older ones are more difficult to handle at first, and he has learned to wear coveralls to protect his legs from their whipping tails.

A black sack can be used if one becomes nasty while being tamed. By putting the sack over its head there is the illusion of night, which dampens its activity while also acting as a muzzle. Mr. Meek suggests this as a taming technique, but he rarely resorts to it. After iguanas are tamed they will no longer bite, whip their tails or try frantically to escape.

When he takes his pet iguanas out, Mr. Meek puts each on a leash and attaches the leashes together. The leashes are a combination of fishing line and swivel fasteners. The iguanas don't seem to mind the leashes and he can keep track of them while they are being held by inquisitive passers by. He does not sense any familiarity on the part of the iguanas toward him; when passed to another person, they rarely seem to notice that they are no longer with him. If the person who is holding them handles them properly, they will demonstrate the same behavior as to their owner; for instance, they will curl around one's neck if the temperature is low, as a snake will do.

But the response the iguana shows seems to be related to food and comfort and not to affection either toward each other or toward human beings. Only once did one of his iguanas come to his bed in the morning, and it seemed to answer to its name on occasion. Yet none of his pets consistently respond to his moving about. Once a girl took one of his iguanas, laid down on her back and whispered to it. It apparently responded to her and stayed with her. He feels he has accomplished the same thing by his talking to them and caring for them, but he admits that their behavior baffles him.

Occasionally Mr. Meek's smallest iguana will sit on top of the middle-sized iguana. Maybe this fills a need for warmth or security. The middle-sized iguana shows no outward sign of affection, irritation or even awareness of the smaller one's presence. Their actions defy any interpretation in terms of human emotion.

John Meek sees no behavioral difference between the sexes and, since they are mostly juveniles, no structural differences either, but from what he has read, he feels that he has two of one sex and one of the other. Mr. Meek has never seen iguanas complete a courtship ritual. Once he witnessed one biting another, then dropping its dewlap and bobbing its head up and down. (The dewlap is a flap of skin and does not bloat out as with a frog.) The one receiving the attention simply turned away as if annoyed. Mr. Meek stated that he knows of no naturally hatched iguanas in the United States, but he has heard that some incubated eggs have been brought into the country and have hatched, and the young are reported to have survived.

Like the chameleon, they are able to change color, but the changes are not as rapid nor as drastic. They will be a brilliant green when they are among leaves in the sun. In the dark, the green becomes duller and there are random dark spots. At times the inner sides of their legs have some orange. They are always shades of yellows, reds, greens, and black, never blue.

An iguana's needs are simple; therefore their care is quite straightforward. Every morning Mr. Meek feeds his iguanas hibiscus flowers by hand. The 1½-year-old (body length, excluding tail, 6") eats two or three flowers daily; the 2½-year-old (body length 7½") eats five to seven flowers daily; and the 3½-year-old (body length 10½") eats ten to fifteen. Or, he will feed all three of them one whole banana, and that is sufficient for one day. (That is, the 3½-year-old eats approximately one half banana for that day.) He has never attempted to feed them any meat; he sees no reason to. They drink very little water, but on a hot day they will sleep in the water dish. He provides clean water at all times. If they are out on the lawn they might eat broad-leaved grass, but never narrow-leaved. Generally they will not forage if fed regularly. Some iguanas will not eat in

The chuckwalla, *Sauromalus obesus*, varies considerably in color from very pale to almost black. Some of this variation is due to differences between subspecies from different areas, but some is an adaptation to background tones. Photo by J.K. Langhammer.

This side view of a male *Basiliscus basiliscus* shows the highly developed "sails" or "fins" on the back and tail in this species. Its light weight and great speed actually allow it to run across water for a short distance. Photo by H. Hansen, Aqaurium Berlin.

Lizards commonly climb over or perch on top of each other without showing any reaction. The specimen on top is an *Iguana iguana*, the one on the bottom is a *Ctenosaura*. Photo by G. Marcuse.

captivity and must be force-fed. This is accomplished by exerting pressure on the corners of its mouth and gently forcing in small quantities of food.

The shedding of skin is spasmodic. It flakes and peels in bits and pieces like sunburn. Mr. Meek figures they shed completely approximately four times a year. After they come out of the water, in the process of drying, they seem to shed more than at other times.

Occasionally iguanas have been imported from Central America with mouth rot. Mr. Meek has heard that they are sometimes captured with tranquilizer darts, but more probably the children capture most of them in their hands. For the pet trade they are captured at any age and bagged, then put into cages. In their attempts to free themselves, their noses get caught between the bars and their mouths get bruised and prone to infection. There is an aureo- or polymycin that is on the market which he uses for mouth rot. While they are sore-mouthed, he feeds them prepared baby food vegetables through a mustard dispenser or eye dropper, depending upon their size. It seems that they still have an appetite but the food must be beyond the sore spot on the mouth before they will consume it.

They often come into the country with white mites and ticks. For the mites, he uses a foot powder or a commercial preparation. He uses tweezers to pull off the ticks.

Iguanas are very clean. They have never done any damage to Mr. Meek's house. They never defecate where they dwell. If fed regularly, they will excrete regularly. Once a day they will come down off the valances, where they spend most of their time, and he will let them outside. They will relieve themselves, as he says, "similar to a chicken": liquid and solid at the same time. Afterward they will throw their hips out to the side and walk away so that their tails never drag in their excrement. Iguanas are quite "double jointed" and can reach just about any part of their body with their claws to remove dead skin or relieve an itch. Mr. Meek helps their peeling and trims their toenails, but that is about it for care after the initial removal of skin parasites.

Well cared for iguanas make interesting, unusual, and safe pets; their
main disadvantage is their lack of responsiveness to human attention.
Photo by John Dommers.

Iguanas require no special caging and make themselves at home with ordinary furniture, climbing on chairs and sleeping on tables. They can be rather hard on drapes and tablecloths, however. Photo by John Dommers.

From Mr. Meek's experience, he has noticed that the iguana's escape mechanisms seem to be their strongest instinct. They prefer to escape rather than defend. They will swim like a snake with their legs streamlined against their body. They will climb a tree, preferably over water. They can jump long distances and apparently use their tails to push themselves off.

Another escape mechanism is that the tail will come off in extreme stress. All three of Mr. Meek's iguanas are missing parts of their tails. Accidentally, he once stepped on one's tail and it started to run away, leaving a part of the tail behind. As he picked up the iguana, it whipped what was left of the tail around, and its dewlap dropped. He held it firmly while talking to it and soothing the top of its head, and within two minutes it was calm. The stub bled a couple of drops but there was no demonstrable sign of pain. He is a "softy" and put a little antibiotic and a bandage on it, but he inferred it really wasn't necessary. Afterward, when the iguana attempted a jump it would fall far from its goal, and it took a long while before it was able to judge its new jumping ability. Within seven months the tail had regenerated two inches, and it will probably continue to grow. Probably it will not reach its previous proportions, and the new portion will be entirely black.

If it is cornered or trapped, an iguana may bite, leaving a very clean cut, or use its tail as a whip, which can leave a nasty welt. He has never observed the iguanas using their claws for anything but holding on and climbing, although he mentioned that they might claw to get out of a bag. He considers the iguana to be a "climber by instinct," meaning that they are more apt to go up than to get down. They have a preference for wood over metal, probably because wood is easier for climbing.

Iguanas seem to have an innate fear of dogs but of no other normally encountered animal. Their dewlap will drop if one is nearby, and they will try to get away. This is only if the dog is within sight. But this fear can be overcome—one of his iguanas used to ride on the back of his chihuahua.

At the time of the interview, Mr. Meek had all three iguanas living peacefully together. He has never witnessed any fighting or territorial defense. Once they have established a perch and a source of food, they will spend most of their time in these areas. They will not range over a large area as a seabird will. For instance, his iguanas are allowed free use of the house, but spend most of their time on the valance over the windows.

On one occasion, Mr. Meek's iguanas had been in the car traveling for two months. After one month they would return to the car by themselves. They still continue to do it now when they are not at home. He considers it a survival pattern and habit since their food and comfort was related to the car after a month.

During the day, the iguanas often sit outside on the trellis. Once one had broken out of its harness while we were away, and after about two minutes he had found it, peering over the top of his trailer. This was the farthest he had ever seen one stray—maybe fifty feet. Of course it was still on his property and possibly that could be the determining factor. So he went up on the roof, picked it up with no resistance and threw it down to me—a sight to behold. It spread its four legs wide and landed in my out-stretched arms gently, without digging with its claws in the least. It climbed onto my shoulder, I soothed the top of its head and it soon had climbed onto my head where it had perched itself in the past.

The iguanas will lie in the sun on their stomachs with their forelegs up against their sides. If the temperature drops below 70° F. they will huddle together and Mr. Meek·brings them inside. If they get colder, they will become inactive and go into torpor. They will slowly die if it becomes too cold. They are daylight creatures and become inactive in the dark.

The iguana is an affable creature. It is quiet and clean; it makes no unexpected demands, does not need a cage, does not breed like rabbits. They will never leave their home. They cannot disappoint their owner.

Mr. Meek finds his pets an interesting challenge and enjoys working with them. They don't demand his time but seem to thrive and become tamer as he cares for them. Clues to their behavior challenge him and their habits and appearance are a great conversation piece.

Unlike snakes, iguanas shed their skin in small patches over a long period of time. Photo by John Dommers.

Although not social, pet and wild iguanas both seem to lack any real aggressiveness toward others of their species, even under rather trying conditions. Photo by John Dommers.

FOOD

The iguana is smart. He selects his food to provide a balanced diet. If this is what you believe—great!

The iguana is stupid, but providentially he is endowed with a very tolerant digestive system. Perhaps this is what you believe—great!

Here are a few *facts* about your iguana which might be useful regardless of which statement you believe.

Young iguanas in the wild are known to eat insects, small animals, birds, other reptiles, land snails, fruit, vegetables, flowers and buds. Adult wild iguanas have been found with some animal food in their stomachs. Other adults have been known to thrive in the wild on a 100% vegetarian diet.

Iguanas are rarely seen to drink, but they do like to bathe and swim and soak; perhaps they do drink or absorb moisture through their skin. The Galapagos land iguana eats or licks plants wet with dew and also seems to drink sea water.

Iguanas consume some gravel which they use in their alimentary canals to aid in breaking up tough vegetable matter.

One fine specimen of common iguana contributed to the Staten Island Zoo in New York was reported to have thrived on mozzarella cheese and ice cream. At the zoo it thrived on the regular iguana diet.

Another, a pet in Washington, D.C., ate vegetables for twelve years and is thriving. This specimen has a special fondness for frozen spinach souffle, served piping hot! He is known to drink water from time to time. His owner believes that the preference for vegetables over fruit may have been acquired since vegetables were all he got to eat when he was a baby twelve years ago.

Specialized foods are now manufactured primarily or exclusively for iguanas. Photo courtesy of Fluker Farms.

Food cubes available in fruit and flower or vegetable formula are suitable for the herbivorous lizard. Photo courtesy of Ocean Nutrition.

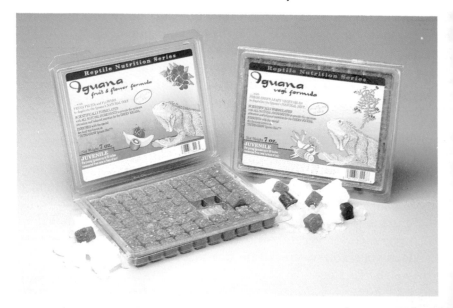

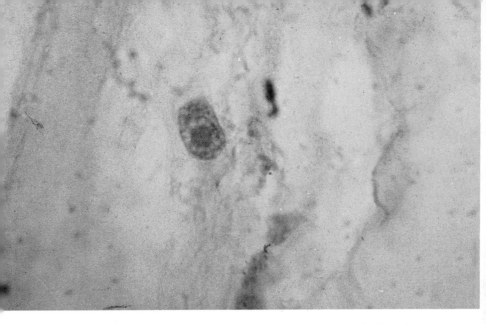

The presence of unusual protozoans, such as this *Amoeba invadens,* in the digestive tract can result in diarrhea and other digestive ailments. Photo by Dr. E. Elkan.

The small nematode worm *Capillaria* may lodge in the smaller blood vessels and produce obstructions leading to the death of surrounding tissue and eventual death of the lizard. Such a condition is rare, however. Photo by Dr. E. Elkan.

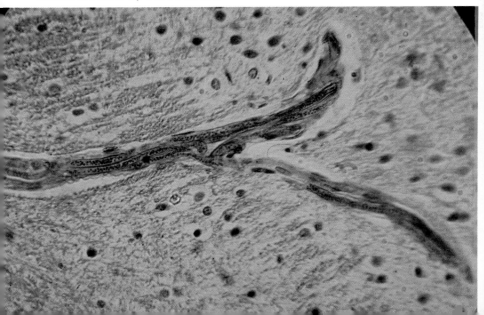

Mr. Meek feeds his pets hibiscus flowers and ripe bananas, but no animal food.

Perhaps you would do well to offer your pet a variety and let him choose. Try fresh peas and beans, canned, frozen or, better still, fresh fruits and vegetables. Canned dog or cat food might be a good source of calcium for bone growth. Cod liver oil with Vitamin D added might be a good tonic if no *direct* sunlight is available. Iguanas can probably generate their own Vitamin D if they are able to bask in direct sunlight or in the rays of an ultraviolet sun lamp perhaps a half-hour daily. Don't cook your pet. Provide shade for him to crawl into if the light is too strong or too long. Perhaps a liquid multivitamin preparation in an oil emulsion spread on his fresh vegetables or fruit would be easier for you to manage than the ultraviolet light. Remember however that a cold-blooded *cold* iguana cannot properly digest his food. He should never be cooler than 65°, and for at least a few hours daily he should be permitted to warm up to 85°-100° —*if he wishes*. The food will do no good if the animal is too sluggish to digest it.

Your pet might begin to lose his appetite for daily meals after he reaches a weight of perhaps ten pounds. Then he might prefer to eat a good meal every other day or perhaps only every third day. Many zoo lizards are fed this way and they live long and healthy lives.

Elsewhere in this book there is a reference to the salty liquid which an iguana snorts out of his nostrils from time to time. You would do well to offer your pet some salted food as an option so that he can make up the salt loss and provide for a natural turnover. Ordinary table salt sprinkled on *some* of his food will give him the chance to select it if he senses the need. Sea salt might be better because it contains trace elements. This latter is speculation and is not the documented results of any research.

You might offer a young iguana crickets, grasshoppers, mealworms and very young mice, and maybe he will add them to his fruit and vegetable bill-of-fare. Or maybe he will just settle down to frozen spinach souffle, served hot.

HANDLING

The iguana is not an affectionate household pet. He is attractive, odorless, long-lived, undemanding, quiet, all these, yes. But affectionate, no. He doesn't relish being picked up. He will permit you to carry him. He will perch on your shoulder if he is cold and your shoulder is warm, but he will not come to you for companionship. You might train him to come for food or for help when patches of skin don't shed easily, but that is about the limit.

So what is there to handling? Several precautions: Don't pick up an iguana by its tail. It is his weapon and also his escape mechanism. If he is frightened he will use his tail as a whip or a flail and, failing this, he will drop his tail to facilitate an escape. Either way, if you grasp your iguana's tail, you are inviting trouble. Support your pet under his front legs and abdomen. Lift him this way only when necessary. Tame your pet as Mr. Meek tames his, and then enjoy him for what he is, but don't expect him to cuddle like a cat or lick you like a puppy. No way.

Some thoroughly domesticated pet iguanas do seem to enjoy having their heads rubbed. Perhaps this is one place they cannot conveniently reach, and if yours enjoys this and you enjoy it also, good.

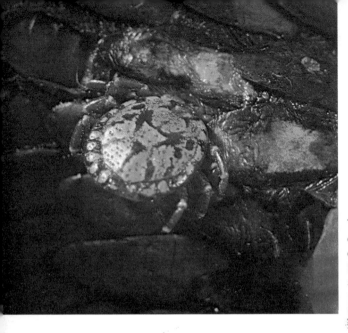

Ticks often come in on wild-caught iguanas, but they are seldom a real problem. Photo by Dr. E. Elkan.

Feeding your iguana or other pet lizard the wrong foods can result in a condition called fatty degeneration of the liver. The liver cells cease to function in digestion and the animal wastes away and dies. Photo by Dr. E. Elkan.

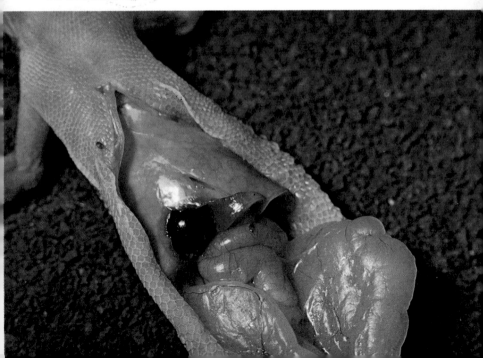

When most small iguanas are found in the petshop they have badly scarred or even bloody snouts from attempts to escape. If carefully cared for they will recover rapidly, but there is always the chance of a dangerous fungus infection setting in. Photo by Dr. Herbert R. Axelrod.

HOUSING

The ideal situation is a tropical tree overhanging a slowly moving tropical stream. Maybe you will settle for a shelf four feet long and eight or ten inches wide over a bookcase. Access can be by a rough-barked tree limb from the floor. Your pet will learn to climb down the limb to get to his food, water, bath and his place to defecate, and then back up to digest and contemplate and perhaps bask in the sunlight or artificial warmth and light you provide. The shelf and limb or arrangement of limbs can also be placed in a cage or a large aquarium. The cage should be long enough for your pet to stretch out his full length, wide enough so he can turn around easily and high enough to permit him to climb.

The cage, aquarium or room should be heated so it never gets cooler than 68° or 70° and located where, each day, your pet can bask in sunlight or its equivalent at temperatures between 80° and 100°. He will probably settle for a steady 70° at night and a minimum of 80° to 85° during the day. *He knows* when he is comfortable. Give him the range and see what he chooses. You need not heat his entire cage or room every day, but you should provide an animal heater pad or a light over a perch where he can warm up if he wishes. Be sure he is never *forced* to remain under a hot light or on a heating pad.

His other requirements are simple. He needs food and a dish to eat it from. Also gravel for his digestive system. Offer a variety of sizes and he will choose the particles he craves. Water to drink, even if he rarely does, is a necessity (perhaps an occasional offering of weakly salty water also), water to bathe in at the same temperature range as the air, and finally some papers to defecate on. You can, with intelligent patience, establish his pattern for eating, then bathing, then defecating, and even with your pet free in one or two rooms of your home he can still be "housebroken."

If you create a cave for within the cage, it should be fastened securely to its parts and also to the cage itself. Avoid jagged edges and sharp corners. Your pet may have no trouble in a vast forest with one or two sharp rocks or wires or boards with splinters, but when he spends twenty-four hours a day in the same place, these hazards will become sore irritants—literally.

An iguana in a tropical rain forest is wet once a day during the rainy season, and yet here in this very same sentence we tell you to "avoid constant humidity." The explanation is simple. A cage or tank which has been dampened remains damp indefinitely, but a treetop which gets rained upon for thirty minutes is dry within the next thirty and remains so until the next rainstorm. Bacteria and fungi which cause skin lesions and blisters on lizards require warmth and moisture. The moisture must be ever present to support the organisms; so a thirty minute wash gives the lizard a chance to soak up or drink a little moisture and then the next twenty-three hours and thirty minutes of dry time keep the fungus and bacteria under control.

If your pet is kept in a well ventilated cage, then a spray every day or every other day might be great, but without the chance for him to dry off thoroughly, you are inviting trouble with humidity.

The temperature requirements for the common green iguana have been studied by Dr. Joel Wallach, and his report in the *Journal of the American Veterinary Medicine Association* (159:1632-1643; 1969) suggests an extreme range of 79.7° F. to 108.5° F. for active reptiles. The preferred ideal range is 85.1° to 103.1° F. and the critical or lethal high temperature is 114.8° F. In other words, your pet will enjoy basking in the direct sunlight but you *must* provide him with a shady escape if he finds it too much.

Physignathus lesueuri is an agamid lizard (not an iguanid) likely to be confused with iguanas. This is an Old World lizard which differs only in details of the teeth and scalation from the New World iguanas. Photo by H. Hansen, Aquarium Berlin.

There are a number of substrates available. Iguana keepers can choose from a bark material, available in bulk, which is easy to work with as well as a terrarium lining which is fully washable and mildew resistant. Photos courtesy of Four Paws.

Fluorescent bulbs for lighting iguana housing units are available at pet shops in varying wattages and spectra. Photo courtesy of Coralife/Energy Savers.

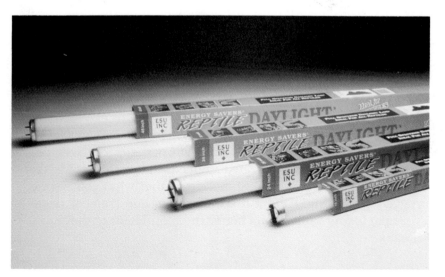

COLD-BLOODED?

From the time of Aristotle through Linnaeus and even more recently, the classes of animal life were described as warm-blooded or cold-blooded. Unfortunately for describers of animal life who like to simplify, there is no absolute black and no absolute white in nature. All life is full of shades of gray. Mammals that hibernate do so with body temperatures much lower than their normal operating temperature. This goes for the bear and the woodchuck and doubtless many others.

Among reptiles the temperature regulation is managed by their behavior. A cool snake will bask in the sun or partially bury itself in warm sand. An overheated lizard will seek shade or a burrow. Perhaps additional study will show that.when the Indian python incubates her eggs she is actually providing some temperature regulation as well. If thermo-regulation is necessary for reptile health (and this does seem to be the case), and this regulation is behavioral, then the pet keeper is duty bound to provide the environment in which his pet can behave to suit his temperature requirements. Nothing profound about that, but it is up to you to furnish a heat source with basking areas at various distances from it and also a shadow area where your pet can escape if the heat gets to be too much. All this can easily fit into a cage. Mount a light at the top, then several shelves or branches at various distances and then perhaps you will discover that the shadows created under the shelves provide the cool escape areas as well. Just make sure that what you erect is rugged and stable. A light that falls down and traps or burns your pet is *your* fault. Don't blame the stupid light or the stupid iguana.

DISEASES

There are a few diseases of interest to the iguana keeper. Some are also mildly dangerous to man, but most can be cured if treated promptly.

External parasites are probably the first "diseases" you will encounter. These are ticks, chiggers and mites. Once eliminated from a newly acquired pet, they should be gone forever. Here's how: Ticks and chiggers resemble ticks and chiggers found on dogs. Pick them off with tweezers. Try to get their heads when you pull them loose. Chiggers and small ticks are hard to find. Watch a new specimen and keep picking if necessary. Since these ticks are probably a tropical species, once they are finally eliminated your pet should be free. Some people think that some lemon juice or alcohol or vinegar or tobacco juice helps in getting ticks to release their grip. This may be so, but generally a gentle slow tug with tweezers will suffice.

Mites are tiny, so small you probably can't see them, but they are a great vexation to your iguana and should be eliminated promptly. Mites leave a fine dust of their white droppings on the lizard's skin, or perhaps you can see them scurrying about, especially on his neck or head.

A total immersion in warm water and transfer into a freshly scrubbed cage will probably rid your pet of adult mites, but there will be eggs to hatch out later. Try the water, but if it doesn't work, don't give up. Try Sulphanone, an insecticide, or Dri-Die 67, a dehydrating agent. The Sulphanone is a poison to mites but harmless to reptiles. Dri-Die 67 is a dehydrating agent and kills mites by drawing all the moisture out of them. Either of these medications should be dusted on your pet and allowed to remain for twelve to eighteen hours. Then wash off

The large *Hydrosaurus amboinensis* is another agamid lizard resembling the iguanas. Found in the western Pacific islands, this partially aquatic lizard has a crest much like that of the basilisk. Photo by H. Hansen, Aquarium Berlin.

Reptiles in general and iguanas in particular have achieved a popularity great enough to allow manufacturers to make specialized foods, food supplements and other products widely available on a commercial basis. Photo courtesy of Coralife/Energy Savers.

Often seen in petshops are small tegus, *Tupinambis*, a South American relative of the common North American racerunners (family Teiidae). If they survive to adulthood, tegus may exceed four feet in length; the tail of an adult is a powerful weapon and they are often in a mood to use it. Few tegus make good pets. Photo by H. Hansen, Aquarium Berlin.

the powder with a warm bath and several rinses and clean the cage thoroughly before reintroducing the specimen.

These two insect killers should be available through your pet dealer or veterinarian. A mixture of half-and-half castor oil and 90% grain alcohol brushed on the affected areas may also eliminate mites. Don't dip your pet in this mixture; just apply a little locally. Note that 90% grain alcohol is not 90 proof. You can buy 90% grain neutral spirits in your pharmacy or liquor store. A little goes a long way.

If you pick off ticks and chiggers with the tweezers, you might well follow up with an alcohol swab to help reduce the risk of infection at the sore spot. Perhaps a pretreatment with the alcohol will tend to loosen the tick before you attempt to pick it off. This passage is not intended to scare anyone from keeping an iguana. People have had dogs and cats with chiggers, ticks, mites and fleas for all of the recorded history of

A number of large and small ticks attached under the edges of the scales of a rainbow boa. The ticks found on iguanas are usually similar in appearance to those found on snakes — ticks are not too choosy. Photo by G. Marcuse.

mankind; but since iguanas are relatively new to us as pets, many people might miss the significance of a lump, a white or grey dust or the lackluster appearance of an iguana suffering from one or several of these parasites.

A warm, sunny, dry perch with no cracks or openings which might harbor a hiding parasite will go a long way to eliminating this problem. If you are thorough and careful there should never be a problem. Incidentally, Dri-Die 67 is not a drug but rather, as mentioned before, a dessicant. It is silica gel with the water removed. When it is sprinkled or dusted on a surface it draws off the surface moisture. It literally dries off the parasite. The problem is that with a small and possibly weakened iguana the treatment will also tend to dry out the host animal and may kill him, too. Experience will help you here. If this is your first pet iguana and he has mites, you might well take him to your veterinarian and suggest that *he* read this chapter before he prescribes a treatment for your pet.

One more word about Dri-Die—the dust may be inhaled by the lizard and too much of this is dangerous since it could lead to lung diseases. Consider Dri-Die as a one-shot treatment rather than a thing you will repeat. Once you rid the animal and the cage of mites and mite eggs, you should not be troubled with them again.

The final answer to mites, ticks and chiggers might be a plastic insecticide strip or perhaps a piece from your dog's flea collar suspended in the cage for one week every couple of months or so if there is a chance of re-infestation. This technique has been used successfully.

Do not use DDT in any form in or around reptiles; even small doses are frequently lethal.

Another class of problems often encountered with captive reptiles is nutritional. The owner finds that lettuce and hamburger meat are convenient for *him* and, since the pet eats to keep from starving, everything looks rosy for a few months. It cannot continue indefinitely because the iguana (for example) needs more calcium than phosphorus in his diet. Actually, about one to one and a half parts calcium to one part phosphorus, and this just isn't available in lettuce and hamburger. In addition, the problem is often aggravated by a lack of Vita-

Another South American teiid lizard is the largely aquatic *Dracaena guianensis*. This large and cumbersome lizard lives along the margins of streams and small rivers and feeds on a variety of aquatic life, especially large snails. It is uncommon and seldom survives in captivity very well. Photo by H. Hansen, Aquarium Berlin.

In addition to iguanids, agamids, and some teiids, the other large lizards commonly seen as pets or in petshops are the varanids, all in the genus *Varanus* of the family Varanidae. These are Old World lizards of very large size, great strength, and often mean dispositions. The Komodo dragon is a species of *Varanus*. Shown here is the common and somewhat smaller (but still more than four feet long) *Varanus salvator*. Photo by H. Hansen, Aqaurium Berlin.

min D which is necessary for the animal to assimilate what calcium he does consume. Bones soften, deformities develop and death results.

The control is easy. It is why you are a pet keeper. Just broaden the diet, especially with rapidly growing juveniles. If you acquire a really rundown specimen, take him to your veterinarian for an emergency injection of calcium gluconate.

Then you should push the Vitamin D. Oil his food slightly with irradiated cod liver oil. (Multiple vitamins such as Parke-Davis ABDEC are also effective here.) Also feed him powdered calcium supplement dusted on his food. Dust by the "Shake and Bake" technique.

Finally, once he is over the hump, you should change his diet to include more Vitamin D, more calcium, more variety. A juvenile iguana might be tempted to eat crickets, mealworms, whole small mice, dandelion flowers, roses, and a good grade of canned dog food now and then.

The Vitamin D need not come from cod liver oil or vitamin drops if direct sunlight—not through glass—or a "Grolux" type fluorescent light is available. Your pet can make his own Vitamin D if he has sunlight or an equivalent. This ultraviolet (UV) light was also mentioned in the housing chapter, but it is so important it bears repeating.

Another diet problem can develop if you let your pet get on an animal organ eating kick. If all you feed him is chicken liver and kidneys, for instance, he will eventually suffer from gout. So would you. Offer your pet whole organisms when he is young and growing up.

Another iguana health problem is mouth rot. This is an infectious disease following an injury in a run-down specimen. Often the animal dies from starvation because he cannot eat while suffering from the disease. Symptoms are yellow patches, yellow crust and cottony substances on the jaws or gums. Treatment includes antibiotics such as penicillin ointment rubbed on infected areas and penicillin administered orally or injected. Your veterinarian should be consulted, especially since most penicillin drugs are not readily available without a prescription anyway.

Still another iguana killer is respiratory disease. Generally it is found in run-down specimens. Buy a healthy animal and take good care of it and avoid this problem. If you are the owner of a thin-tailed, grey, wet-eyed or sunken-eyed snuffler who doesn't eat or distend his dewlap or otherwise show an enthusiasm for life, you might try several cures simultaneously:

Try a penicillin-type drug administered by your veterinarian.

Provide sunlight, preferably direct and unfiltered by glass.

Coax food — try variety.

Avoid handling and stressing the animal.

Keep temperature up—say 82° F. to 90° F. both day and night during the treatment.

Keep cage dry and clean. Clean means antiseptically clean. Wash the cage with a carbolic acid preparation like Lysol and then thoroughly rinse and dry it to assure that no chemical remains before placing the animal back in his quarters.

Avoid wooden cages and cages with complicated construction where parasites and germs can hide and avoid detection and disinfection.

It should be noted that some iguana parasites pass through complicated life cycles and during one stage may leave a reptile and find a bird or mammal host, possibly even a human. The important thing to remember is that the parasites like chiggers, ticks and mites sometimes carry within their systems such diseases as "Q" fever. When a mite carrying "Q" fever infests an iguana then the iguana becomes a stepping stone for the disease to be transmitted further.

The control is simple. Free your iguana from ticks, chiggers and mites. Keep the iguana isolated from other animals which might transfer new infestations. Keep the cage clean. Sterilize it if necessary. Keep the cage simple so that parasites do not have a place to hide while you are eliminating the individuals clinging to your pet. Once freed of parasites your new acquisition need never be infested again.

This adult *Varanus salvator* displays the heavily clawed forelimbs, long neck, and slender head characteristic of the varanids. The claws and tail can inflict serious damage. Varanids are not suitable for the average pet keeper. Photo by H. Hansen, Aquarium Berlin.

The common American green anole, *Anolis carolinensis*, looks much like an iguana in miniature. One of numerous North American iguanids, the anole is easily recognized by widened finger and toe pads which allow it to climb vertical surfaces. Photo by G. Marcuse.

Not all mites are found on the exposed skin of your reptile pet. Some species get into the nostrils, others get into the trachea and lungs. This is a job for your veterinarian. Others lodge themselves near the sometimes moist area near the cloaca and around the base of the tail. This you can clear up by drying and disinfecting the cage.

Occasionally a recently imported iguana is found which is free of mites and ticks but is still wasting away, although eating well. This animal may be suffering from pin worms or other internal parasitic worms. His cloaca will be loaded with them and your veterinarian will be able to find them in the feces in the same way he examines dogs and cats. He may be able to treat your pet successfully. The problem is usually that the pet owner doesn't recognize that there is a problem until the specimen is on the threshold of death.

If you wish to avoid problems like this, start with a bright-eyed healthy animal and keep him clean and isolated from other animals which may be infested with parasites.

Your pet may not wear down his toenails as fast as they continue to grow. If you notice that they are twisting under or corkscrewing, you might do well to prune them a little. Go at it slowly until you find how far to clip without striking living tissue—the part of the nail nearest the toe is actually alive and is supplied with veins, arteries and nerves.

You should use a tool which cuts the nail but does not splinter it by crushing. For a young iguana, perhaps an ordinary fingernail clipper will suffice. Larger lizards will need the tool which is used for dogs. Perhaps you can buy one in your pet shop. You should not ever strike the "quick," but if you do, you can stop the flow of blood with a styptic pencil—this is just alum and is available in your drugstore or from nearly any man who shaves with a razor. As with any minor wound, it can be treated with an antiseptic cream, but it will probably heal uneventfully regardless of whether you treat it or not.

DID YOU KNOW THAT. . .

. . . the first reference to iguanas, dated in 1555, was: "Foure footed beastes. . . named Iuannas, muche lyke unto Crocodiles, of eight foot length, of moste pleasaunte taste." The author was Eden, the title of the work, *Decades*.

. . . in 1617 Sir Walter Raleigh of the cloak in the mud puddle fame stated that "South America hath plenty of. . . Tortoyses, Armadiles, Wanaes."

. . . Captain John Smith of Pocahontas fame had this to say in 1630, "Gwanes they have, which is a little harmlesse beast, like a Crokadell or Alligator, very fat and good meat."

. . . the name of our subject has varied in its spelling through the years according to the Oxford Dictionary (1901). Various authors handled it thus: iuanna, iwana, iguano, yguana, guana, wana, gwane, gwayn, yuana, igoana, hiuana.

. . . the playwright Tennessee Williams (1914-) wrote a three act tragedy entitled "The Night of the Iguana." It is a story woven around the capture of an iguana which was then imprisoned until it was to be eaten, all in a little town on the west coast of Mexico in 1940. The behavior and natural history of the iguana described in the play are of no value to pet keepers. In fact, it is really a play about people with problems.

Horned toads (*Phrynosoma*) are very greatly modified iguanids living in deserts and eating mostly ants. They seldom find the proper conditions in captivity and die within months. Above is the common *P. cornutum*, below the rare and protected *P. solare*. Photos by J.K. Langhammer.

Leiocephalus carinatus and similar species of small curly-tailed lizards are often common on Caribbean islands and are now also found in Florida. Photo by H. Hansen, Aquarium Berlin.

One of the leopard lizards, *Crotaphytus wislizeni* of the western United States is an iguanid that, like the basilisk, can run on its hind legs. It is found in deserts and grassy plains. Photo by J.K. Langhammer.

READING LIST

Beebe, B.F. *American Desert Animals*. David McKay, New York, 1966. Iguanas and coatis. The coati is a racoon-like animal which likes to eat iguanas.

Breen, John F. *Encyclopedia of Reptiles and Amphibians*. T.F.H. Publications, Neptune, N.J., 1974. A copiously illustrated text with a good reading list.

Carr, Archie. *The Reptiles*. Life Nature Library—Time Life Books, New York, 1963. Reptile recipes and much natural history in easily readable form. A good book for a pet keeper to own.

Ditmars, Raymond L. *Reptiles of the World*. Macmillan, New York, 1933. Natural history with remarks about diet and arboreal habits of iguanas.

Figuier, Louis. *Reptiles and Birds*. Cassell, Petter and Galpin, London and New York, 1870. Natural history, much detail not repeated in other books about iguanas and dogs and breeding.

Frye, F.L. *Husbandry, Medicine and Surgery in Captive Reptiles*. V.M. Publishing Co., Bonner Springs, Kansas, 1974. Offers solutions to many problems encountered in keeping reptiles.

Gadow, Hans. *Amphibia and Reptiles*. Macmillan and Co., London, 1909. Descriptions and natural history with remarks about the common green iguana like this, "In going up some of the narrow unfrequented creeks in the Mosquito country, according to Napier Bell, the voyager often encounters quite a shower of falling Iguanas, and runs some risk of getting his neck broken."

Hornaday, William T. *The American Natural History*. Charles Scribner's Sons, New York, 1914. A good library reference by a famous collector and zoo keeper. He makes observations about the common, rhinoceros and marine iguanas.

International Zoo Yearbook, Zoological Society of London, Regents Park, London, NWI 4RY England. Articles about endangered species, longevity and husbandry of reptiles, primarily for zoo keepers.

Lizard Ecology, A Symposium. University of Missouri Press, Columbia, 1965. Behavior, nesting, responses to temperature.

Miller, A.H. and Stebbins, R.C. *The Lives of Desert Animals in Joshua Tree National Monument*. University of California Press, Berkeley, 1964. The natural history of the desert iguana, *Dipsosaurus dorsalis*.

Minton, Sherman A., Jr. and Minton, Madge Rutherford. *Giant Reptiles*. Charles Scribner's Sons, New York, 1973. Sex differences, mating, breeding and interesting sidelights including the sources of warts and mention of a Yankee tourist who purchased a "talking iguana" from a Panamanian ventriloquist.

Reichenbach-Klinke, H. and Elkan, E. *The Principal Diseases of Lower Vertebrates*. Academic Press, London and New York, 1965. Especially valuable for its discussion of parasitic mites and ticks on lizards. This book is also published by T.F.H. Publications.

VanDenburg, John. *The Reptiles of Western North America: Volume I, Lizards*. California Academy of Sciences, San Francisco, 1922. Description of black spiny-tailed and San Lucan spiny-tailed iguanas. Also *Dipsosaurus* species and *Sauromalus*.

The common name "swift" is applied to several western iguanids of small size that are able to run very rapidly. Some are found on the ground, while others climb low shrubs and trees. Above is *Sceloporus clarki,* below is *Uta stansburiana.* Photos by F.J. Dodd, Jr.

Several small iguanids of various genera have become modified for rapid burrowing in the sand and for running across loose desert sands. These often have wedge-shaped heads and long fringing scales on the toes. Above is *Holbrookia maculata*, below is *Callisaurus draconoides.* Photos by F.J. Dodd, Jr.

INDEX: Page numbers set in *italics* indicate illustrations.